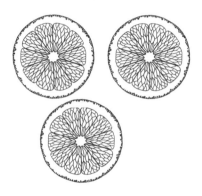

APPLIES to ORANGES

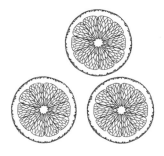

MAUREEN THORSON

Ugly Duckling Presse
Brooklyn, New York 2011

Applies to Oranges
© 2011 by Maureen Thorson
ISBN 978-1-933254-85-2

First Edition 2011
Printed in the USA

Cataloging-in-publication data is available
from the Library of Congress.

Distributed to the trade by
Small Press Distribution
1341 Seventh Street
Berkeley, CA 94710
www.spdbooks.org

Available directly from Ugly Duckling Presse
and through our partner bookstores.

Ugly Duckling Presse
232 Third Street, E-002
Brooklyn, NY 11215
www.uglyducklingpresse.org

I have always thought of poetry as a way of building a world
. . . not better, but other.

—*Rosmarie Waldrop*

I'd rather tell you a better story, but
disease and boredom and a bad connection
brought that plan to night. You took off
with the oranges and spiders,
the ending and the plot, and left me
with the Zenith's chrome housing,
the cruise ships in their moorings.
The tender tourists with their trinkets
and tight-fisted maps. The orphans
and beachheads, so lovelorn and solemn.
The satellites' red signals. The hotel's
common gestures. Once you were gone,
there were only these few things left.

High in soft mountains, where indigo
is the color of shadow, spiders crawl.
In that place, there is no purpose,
but there is a system that sends me
to the porch at daybreak to watch the mist
dissolve over what used to be oranges,
where I hear the Zenith's test pattern drowned
in birdsong, in the shadow of some shift
in the system. Blue signifiers—the ocean,
its downbeats, its tides that spiral and glide.
You once read them as instructions: *Escape.*
If I'd known what "escape" signified.

A history provisionally set
with high-voltage rays, the sensation
of sailing a river that never moved.
Those days were badly tied together,
they fell apart like tiles, and now
when women thunder through cafes
made of daubed mud, electric wires
clutched fiercely between their teeth,
I can answer only with a peculiar
gesture of loss—flexing and dipping
my hand as though it held something
with a sure trajectory, an orange,
perhaps, a stone.

Rain again, and no oranges.
Hysteria's minor text, a soft accretion.
Once, rain made this house the playground
of spiders: scuttled by storms, they wove
in cupboards, settled in Sunday shoes.
Banana spiders roosted in the eaves,
crab spiders worked their warped shells,
plying rainy-day crafts while we watched
droplets cast shadows on the wavy windowglass.
And if our silken factory housed any tension,
it was obscured by its own diligent surface,
the gloss edge of an aqueous light.

My voice a faltering promontory.
When I stutter, watch out below.
Echoes are my kind of arguments,
stormclouds birthing a muffled doppler,
acoustics unsuitable to reason.
Appeals to the angelic. Exactly why
my voice, recounting the past, sounds
a bit like rosaries slipping over,
why an orange sows only oranges,
carbon copies of every memory,
degrading a little with each retelling,
these things that burst and burn.

At first, heartbreak made me beautiful.
My skin fluoresced. I hypnotized trees.
The orphans followed me around town,
drunk on my pain. I ate only my own
hunger, gave off a scent like bitter oranges
or chlorine. Loss left me strangely whole,
as if my sadness, were it strong enough,
could turn your ship around. That was back
when I aged. Now, like an astronomer
who seeks no first causes, but only to map
the connections pinned out over the sea,
I want to diagram the light that shines out
through the holes you pricked into me.

The Zenith's reruns are interrupted
by a bulletin about the orphans' newest scheme:
turning the rusty wharves into a perfect replica
of an ancient Roman forum. The anchor
has a nervous tic, the director must be colorblind—
all those dots and checks and "Back to you, Manuel."
Peculiar choices. I've got the basic plot—
boy meets girl, orphan meets idea,
and something happens, happy or sad.
But why each of these particular things?
Why did we hunger on for years?
Why the orange tie, Manuel?

The ship's propeller churns the rough.
Say good-bye, wave your hanky at it.
The monogram on the starched linen—
HRH. Everything turns over again.
The moon eyes the paint that marks
the waterline like a gangster eyes a mirror:
it knows if its scars are right. You catch
the edge of a white dress as it hurries
off the deck, trailing the faintest scent
of oranges. If you come home, I won't
be waiting. The wind shifts. Spiders trapped
in the portholes are calling out your name.

A fox-shaped car rolls through
fog-cozened gates. My Zenith
lays its mysteries bare in black
and white: the butler, the turret,
the pomanders of clove-studded oranges.
When the mistress of the house
comes in from the damp mist that rises
out of the river, stripping her gloves
like an impertinent skin, her sere mouth
ready to insult whomever she sees
over her shoulder, I can picture the eyes
behind the knife already, soft as flowers,
stamens nodding with a silvery glint.

I repeat myself, but every repetition
is imperfect. In the spaces between
stutters, in the halts between each
forward move, there may be room
in which we can, say, enter persona.
Enter mother-in-law. Enter psycho
killer qu'est-ce que c'est. Or no,
enter only endless nights over which
to remember incipient oranges,
the buds creeping open in darkness,
the scent that sparks regression,
how the bloom went on for miles.

This is how stalagmites build, how meaning
explodes, and the camel's back becomes
a bower heady with oranges. Brides
came for miles to cut crowns of blossoms
from my orchard's boughs, but now
not even spiders mate here, and the air
contains only satellites, machines
sending sounds to other machines.
Twilight reflects terrible intentions—
the cord's been cut from the phone.
If there's a problem from here on,
Houston, you'll have to go it alone.

Dogs bark on a barge on the river at night.
The birds are hiding again, getting thin
in the fractured dark. Tonight's feature
presentation: '50s B-grade sci-fi, complete
with theremin. Chrome knobs chipped,
the Zenith at its perigee. Once you got dizzy
just staring. Back when the oranges
were small, reedy trees too young to fruit.
Now they're gone and the birds shiver,
the dogs howl all night, as though monsters
were seeping out of the river, hands
dripping with futures long past.

What if I were a ghost, dead as the oranges
that line the river we only cross once?
Would I wander, transparent and weightless,
from the graveyard and over the sea, through
walls and mountains, to find you, to watch
you stalk and revolve your earthly scene?
Rap on your table? Throw flowerpots off
your windowsills, and trace greetings in
the dirt? Would you know me? Could we
shake on it after all? Or would my signal
fail to reach you, decay into ornament,
a delicate rustle no meaning may approach?

Morning stumbles into the room
and I think for a moment that spiders
are working a delicate seam
along the trail of my lashes.
Three months on, the stumps
remember being trees, waving in the wind.
Your body's ghost hovers in the sheets,
smelling faintly of oranges.
Blue light embroiders the room
with its afterimages, and I wrap
myself inside them, shimmering
like a photograph I can't put down,
a memory that won't fade away.

In your absence, I've nothing to lose
but tension binding water to moonlight
to oranges floating ghosty in night air.
A trick of multiple exposures
to the island's humid threnodies,
its shanties for all things lost
or barely remembered. A pan of the scene
would reveal only the expected: wood
rotting in insectoid caresses, plastic
tchotchkes grinning in the variable winds
that curl the harbor, the docks where
the orphans snooze at their tables,
bundles beside their ankles, dreaming
of a future that's subject to change.

Shielded from the sun's thick orange blot
by the gazebo, the orphans play noontime games
with false substitutions. *Minions for Onions.*
Fivers for Rivers, and, of course,
The Four Hundred Contemplative Virtues,
a cross between *Yahtzee* and dying.
Next: crybabies in the desert, all outta water,
waiting for a Bedouin breeze. The story
of Peony Parsnip, down-home contender,
juvenile fiction from a century gone by.
As a cruise ship tenders its load
of pale-bottomed passengers, it's all
moth to my mouth, just desserts for deserters,
and the orphans descending the piers
to sell their stories to whomever walks past.

Loosed to their own devices, islanders
seek smaller islands, by which to examine
their predicament in miniature. The English
go to Mallorca, many others to Manhattan,
some here. Where the wine is cheaply better,
cheaply cheap. Where the radio plays
different stations, and you have no radio.
Where kitchens sour with different meats,
the trees turn orange with birds, and where
stalkers walk through uncanny valleys,
peeping over windowsills at river's edge,
their minds hi-res and compulsive:
a backwards, inexorable flow.

Across the river, the horizon curdles.
Birds tuck their heads in their wings.
When darkness deepens, there are lights
in every machine. Their agonizing flicker—
the autobiography of space. The ocean
wrinkles against itself, wrinkles against
oranges it doesn't have, spiders that it does.
It sings birds back to their nests, it calls
satellites to order. The boneless pulsing
that carried you off might return you yet.
The ocean reaches forward. Greased
by the moon's emotionless mechanics,
it sends out a hundred webs.

A pulse on the air. A chopper's blades
let loose the hero's hair. He whirls
toward the sound, his shadow stretched
shallowly along the rocks. In a second,
he'll be aloft, credits streaming down
his handsome face, white words draped
over gray jungle. Endings are always a form
of return. The Zenith clicks to commercial
and flicks its light across the table, where
a hardbacked *Sonnets from the Portuguese*
stands idly tented in its orange binding.
Outside, treefrogs sing their one refrain:
it's night it's night it's night.

Your legions swill down the country lanes,
and toward *mi pobre hacienda*, its
battered lack of oranges. The soldiers
are infected with time: each feels
the night rising like an insect on his skin.
Once, I might have invited them to cool
their tortured nerves in the river's syrup,
listen to the birds' hungry songs, a music
of spirals. But today I will have no visitors.
I am reading up on horticulture and boats.
I am making a plan of attack.

This actress right for screaming—
mouth tremulous, lungs enormous.
When she tilts her tungsten throat,
the sound is marvelous, clear.
The Zenith ripples finely in its wake,
and, orange at their edges, the stars also
tremble toward stillness. So many scripts
for screaming, in fear or in sorrow,
or with anger, a thin drill of noise
that insists the way is clear. I never
shattered glass, but still I screamed
for you. I tried, at least, to resonate.
I shivered until I made you break.

If we had lived a hundred years ago, I'd say
give me washed leather, milliners' pins,
Battenburg lace looped in orange silk.
Let me learn the politics of exclusion—
six hundred threads to the inch. In place
of island chic, a native's pretend servility,
I'd dress to show that sorrow can harden
into a surface more starched than any collar,
more formal than the pleats of a skirt
as its hem dusts a dim corridor. It sets.
It makes creases I'll never press out.

The Zenith revels in shadow's heyday,
saying: farewell, my lovely. The Santa Ana
blows cosmic dust across the valley,
its orange groves, YMCAs. There's
no complaining, but only the same
bungalows and housewives testing
knifepoints against well-lotioned
fingertips. When the storm clouds
appear, scudding before husbands
rattled by the presumption of innocence,
the blood goes out with the breeze,
like you and I and the dusty rest,
with fear and shrieks and feathers,
the flock come home to roost.

The ship. Somewhere under the hull,
fish explore the valley of their names:
pumpkinseed, sheepshead, lookdown.
Kelp tangles in knots, weaving robes
you and I could wear offshore, where
the Zenith keeps lonely watch.
Tonight's instructions are offered
by a young man in a pinstriped suit—
citizens are advised to lock their doors.
The men in orange suits are coming
to spray for insects. Breathe slowly
if at all, the man intones. Something silvers
up the river—a shadow that speaks to no one,
an infestation no one bothers to name.

The politician wins the debate by proving
his opponent will cause a nuclear war.
The voters can't let things end that way,
and in a foreign city, white with tile,
an ad for orange juice puts you in mind
of an island riddled with spiders, the ship
that took you away. You wonder how
that would go down. The anchorman
behind the glass the only one who can
let the world know: coordinates
are programmed. *God help us all.*
In the boiling heat behind your eyelids'
red screens, you see me standing
at the quay. Then your eyelids darken
and the horizon line gives way.

In an alternate timeline, the rain catches us
on our way back home. Our veils survived,
as did the pocked skins of oranges, cast
out of the windows and into the roadway.
This was late. The paths diverged,
and it was the habit of the time to call it
nobody's fault. Somewhere in the future
a ship was waiting, not to sail, but to ride
between islands on rails set into the seabed.
Spiders, we knew, were natural robots,
and as for destiny? This was just the sort
of future we looked forward to.

Today the orphans sell snow globes
from a sack the youngest pats
like a fat, full stomach, while inside it,
square flakes of tinsel fall thick and fast
over a plastic pier, the gazebo in the square,
the whole island made in miniature, and
strangely devoid of people, when really,
the place is full of them: slow, smoky trails
walking in destroyed light, casting
wavy reflections in orange windowpanes
at dusk, never speaking to each other,
silence what preserves them, what keeps
their mammoth tempers iced.

Broadcasting nightly from the river's darkness,
I've got a new call-sign, buddy. Do you read?
Night, call me Orange. Call me Mr. Fiesta.
I'm giving a shoutout to anyone who knows
Morse code, and I'm losing myself in
the Zenith's blue glow, the transceiver's
dim crackle, the endless white words
of the waves. Stretched helpless along
their length and dreaming that your ship
might come to recover my floating body,
bear it away like a prize, a tiny golden fleece.

Toes sunk in the river's black eddy,
I put the finishing touches on my handbook
on the mechanics of gloom. Intended
for future film directors, it shows exactly
how to ratchet up the melancholy
by accumulating neutral symbols.
Cuckoo clocks are comical, but break them,
stuff them with oleander leaves, and the audience
will despair. Why, I myself have been haunted
by the coincidence of orange-oil candles,
foghorns heard miles away, the dried
body of a spider sliding quietly
through the pages of an unfinished book.

Half a world away, the guns say it again.
You might be there now, I think,
falling in the smoke that blurs the screen.
The news gives way to a talk show host
who tells her guest to *let it all out*.
Her voice is carried by the satellites,
who hear all and relay it to the guns below,
the guns whose sights all turn in your direction.
The women on the couch embrace. *Release*.
The applause is drowned by my clicker's
fierce volley. Those thousand repeaters—
forgiveness. One thousand smoking holes.

Say it with flowers. Bottlebrush aplenty.
The balls-out persuasion of a terrible year.
Diamond-hooey. Emerald knick-knack.
No way to say, except by precisely arranged
azaleas, how cozy I've gotten with death.
No decoder ring included. This much, at least,
is clear: equivalent exchange of minerals
won't bring me oranges, either of us closer,
mend any gap. Instead, I retract
into extravagant gestures, diaries, bonfires,
the psycho gloss of wilted blossoms,
dead-eyed stamens stitched in rows.
There's something almost Victorian in how
I've made killing things for you into an art.

The sound of lovers' eyes expiring
in an alley thick with discarded flowers.
Long after I think I've distanced them
to silence, they deposit a crescendo
that zaps the piers with fingers of orange
lightning, halts the orphans in their spiels,
makes the sailors turn their mouths up
into imbecile smiles. We all love
to listen, to put our individual stamps
on the details playing out in the shadow.
I give the woman a birthmark like Atlantis,
the man my own face, and the scent
of dying flowers a lesson in the things
we could do if we started them over again.

Rev your engines: cell to cell,
the body constantly the mind's
reflection. And yes, an innate
vain love of the marvelous may
surrender me yet to those mirrors
flashed off hillsides, to the graffiti
recorded in your eyes. As the years
wash tourists on and off the island,
as the orange stumps decay, I gather
your fallen phrases and soak in them
until my skin is wet with promises
that only one of us believed,
compromises we both held dear.

Miscues in the greenery—can you find
the monkey, can you find the snake?
We all have found the heat mirage
boiling off the pier, the Christmas lights
tangled round the tastiest shrimp shack
in town. We've found cracked gray pictures
gummed in albums, and stripped
them slowly, fed them to a fire
of blue-then-orange flames. We've
all hid our feelings in the greenery
and when the greenery whistled,
we set our phasers to terminate,
and—no quarter asked, none given—
made sure no word escaped.

I halve the rooster's heart again
and when the feathers fly, bronze
in September's low-lying sun, you return
to me in triplicate, big-screen beauty.
I see you striding through the down
and dust, blood spattered on your ankles,
a thin dress folding around your knees.
You've got an orange in each pocket,
and you walk by death with your head
held high, into the house and its shadow.
You've made your peace with sacrifice.
You only want something to keep you going.
Something alive, something that's ready to eat.

Lambing time at the Hotel Cordillera—
all firm flesh and soft angles as young men
the color of graham crackers pad down
the sugar sand to test the waters with their bodies.
The girls, brought here by snowbird parents
for a week of tropical sunshine, sip virgin mimosas
beneath umbrellas—all orange juice and ginger ale—
and the soft laughter that comes from watching
boys, stifling squeals, and sooner or later
hands behind the cabana, eyelashes fluttering
in the old language of fans, saying *yes-please*
and *oh-if-you-would*, that definitive shut-me-and-shake.

Suddenly, the river births frogs.
Mosquitoes take over for the absent
spiders, hovering around the brushpiles
that screen the river. The birds grow
fat again. Unseen directions instruct
everyone to multiply. The Zenith speaks
of meteors like oranges thrown from
terrible heights, best visible in the west.
Cut to a horse opera, the mules' hooves
kicking dust, the hero's paisley bandana
not only clean but starched and pressed.
He looks up from his campfire into a night
that shatters into unnumbered stars.

The rushes shiver with the distant drums
of the Discoteca Ali Baba, latest incarnation
of the orphans' market genius.
Pale-skinned tourists bob and weave
beneath strobing lanterns, the ocean
gleaming off their fishy limbs.
The bass ripples my heart, turns it tender,
just the way you once let your body down
to mine. That was when I opened
like an orange, as a child might open it—
thumbs in, fingers splayed,
and then the whole thing rips apart.

Bats in the tamarind make a ruckus.
Black gum wings stretch to a bubble,
and the leathery leaves twitch
and squawk. Hidden in the branches,
an emerald boa awaits the long squeeze.
If this were a movie, I'd jump
from the sad bat's airless struggle,
cut to a city, a couple in bed,
the sun made your ship's prison.
But there's no escaping this close-up
on the serpent's orange eyes,
narrowed by proximity and hunger,
tight slivers of your reproach
for what I said or failed to say.

This arm, a ship, plunges forward,
finds flesh. Words shaped by blows,
words sliced open, their vowels
hanging limp. These trees the only
witness: ant's-eye view of oranges
piled on the pier, tarred rope,
the orphans' dirty feet. If there's
translation here, it's loose and short
on substance, long on atmosphere—
the wooden planks you walked,
the salt air that caked your nostrils,
your absence—all the little details
I thought blood could make me forget.

Sling my hammock where? Once I suffered
by a fetish for certain words: *Morocco.*
Carbine. Amor. I transposed their letters,
wrote them backwards, let their meanings
slide into one another and I didn't care—
I thought you knew what I meant.
But those words are as distinct as oranges
held in different hands, as their peeled
and sundered segments, vivisected and precise.
I had a secret instead of a message,
a river without an other side.

A break in the line in the sand
turns this beach into an invitation
to make peace with what's present,
to watch the little crabs sidle along,
eyestalks glistening. Gulls hang gently
on currents of air, sand burrs cling
to my feet, but even if the sea
were to roil and give way
to surfaced pods of whales, a bridge
of basking sharks, one streaky orange cloud
rinsed along the backdrop, I'd still be alone
in the aperture of *wishyouwerehere*,
blank postcard of the home I thought you knew.

12 o'clock. The moon's a peeled orange
admiring itself in the darkened river.
There are no sounds. The birds are asleep.
The mosquitoes have fallen away.
My steps on the porch's rotting planks
are muffled by the humid air. I wear
the shadows the porchlight throws
like a gown, stitched and picked
with yellow thread. Even your voice
is quiet for once, cupped inside my skull.
But it won't spill—don't worry.
I heard you the first time, dear.

Orphaned vendors throng the path
from town to the Hotel Cordillera.
Spare change and "sign my guestbook."
O interpreter of images, consider
these orange, blinking texts, constant
beyond the brilliance of test patterns—
melons, sweet berries, mango nectar.
The entrepreneurial orphans accept
hard cash to proffer from buckets
a little something to make the tourists forget
the existence of exchange, its dirty
directions and incipient sound,
a crass whisper like tightening nets.

Good night, pretty birds. The stars
are all aligned. These constellations
appear for nine days only: the Revolutionary,
the Gangster, and at the island's southern tip,
L'manzana d'oro, the heavenly orange.
Birds snuggled up in the trees drop feathers
that slide in mirrored light along the river's
placid surface, the zodiac of a parallel world,
where yours is the sign of the ready,
the fleeting, the missing, and mine
is that of the steady, who don't double or glide,
the ones that the fleeting can't bear.

Waxy fingers lay gray gloves
across the sideboard, shadows
indistinct against the shadow
of the ancient, enormous furniture.
"When you left," he stammers,
"you left behind a style, a way of being
that took me out of myself
and into something like being you."
His fingers—the lightest of all
the gray things in this scene, some
director's trick of lighting, tremble
at a chair's high back, carved
with scrolls and oranges. From off-scene,
there's only silence, dead air bearing
gray light lightly, subtly shifting its weight.

A sultry chorus overturns the river:
satellites singing the binary hymns
of their ancestors, slow murderous
chirrups, ditties without expiration dates,
like war drums, or hunting horns—
all catchy in their way. I resolve to exploit
these mnemonic boxes, their tapes
and reels and electric sparks, to transfer you
from one tune to another, spinning
like an orange into the cosmos,
lonely locus for twisting in the wind,
for recalling all the anger I can sing.

On the stars' needle-sharp points,
someone's written poems confusing
the shape of your face with shelter,
with long years in a besieged country.
Inverted now in the river's black flow,
they read as marching orders: a call
to the lilies and fish, to the spiders
not here to take the message, to
the birds here to fly it home, chalked
in orange on the shaking surface,
not a love song but a reveille,
the demand that I get up and go.

It's less tiring to run than give chase.
I imagine your refuge as the traveler's blur
of blank destinations—guest registers
and time tables, the glassed enclosures
of public space. You look for identifying
monuments, something that might help
make sense of these cathedrals and plazas
and generic cobbled streets where fruit-sellers
stack oranges like fetid tombs, and my love
follows you a little more slowly each day,
like a dog that wants to lie down,
making signs with its tired eyes.

The orange is a sweet fruit. It grows
on a tree. Kiddo, tell me more—how
our lives recede into other people's stories,
how the worm crawls through the apple,
how glass becomes a staple in countries
without laughter. Stories. If you've other
things to tell me, I'm telling you: don't bother.
If you've got a bridge to sell me, let me
sell you the water. This river is no better
than your multiple dead letters, than a blank
cartouche. What's living here's not hatred,
nor is it any cause for worry. But if I see
your face again, I can't say we won't be sorry.

Rumors abound: a foreign orange juice magnate.
The island's febrile economy rebuilt,
its glory revived, its groves resown overnight.
My money's in continued decay but still
I heart the orphans as they steal through
empty fields, their small bodies weighted
with pottery shards, new antiquities
they'll bury and then unearth to sell
to tourists: a high-margin, high-culture past.
Not just for foreign convenience.
A story that gives everyone a cut.

When the sun slinks beneath its covers,
I begin to build life backwards. Take
this advice from the sugar-mamas,
their lavish earrings, incomparable
teeth: it doesn't matter what it does
so long as it looks good. Some say lyrical.
The bowl of oranges in the background
of every jumpcut. An eye to splice
the reel, to discriminate in favor
of the long, slow take. A thousand years'
stock footage. The black wool beret. I begin
with an ending, then reel you back in.
This work not previewed by critics.
Some say lyrical. Some say tour-de-force.

Breaker nine, breaker nine,
this is reggaeton and the mothers
of invention. Imagine the island
ablaze from end to end, the ghosts
smoked out, the sugar sand
carmelized. Moonsnail lacquer,
baked with footprints. That's one way
to seal these memories: five thousand
degrees, ten stories high. A pillar
of fire flying miles out over the ocean,
coloring sunsets orange. A lighthouse
to warn you from the shores you left behind,
the finale you didn't stick around to see.

"Reader, I married him." The major
arcana await me: The Ship. The River.
The Hanging Orange. It's time to quit
the escapism and escape—put in a call
to the satellites, send my body through
the ether of which ideas are ever sensible,
and set it down beside you—my rubber soles
on cobblestones, a cigarette cantilevered
from my stubbled jaw. Tonight, a tenuous
shadow trails you, released from its walls,
neither a ghost nor your double. Not a story.
A man in a trenchcoat, tactile and real.
And at this point, hardly your friend.

Becoming conflicted, I apply
to oranges rules meant for
tangerines, for buffalo wings
and sake. In the middle of the ocean,
I fail to tack into the fretful wind,
to keep my plotted course. Instead,
I rearrange elements, focus on
glottal stops and sibilants,
what sounds convincing,
even if it's not. The stutter
I lost like an orange returns.
Well, yes'm. Yes'm. Yes.

In a role reversal, the dramatis personae
are left to the end of the book. Nameless
shadows and no signifiers, no different
from what you hear each day while
strolling around the pier, where the orphans,
also nameless, have discovered a new racket:
inspirational sayings carved into clam shells.
They hawk their durable lies to every Rolex
that descends a gangplank, start to lose sight
of the locals, treat neighbor and enemy alike.
At end, what I like best are not the names
but the descriptions—Duke of Sienna, Mother
of Earl, the one who keeps going away.

Stripped to the waist, this sailor displays
a beautiful paradise where leaves swirl out,
and where Eve, etched in cobalt, offers
an apple, certainly scarlet and deep.
Tell the satellites they're licked—there's more
meaning here than a billion bits could relay.
And when the sailor leaves, his meaning
will stay behind in a world that compasses
no destruction, the same world where
the oranges remain. Where nothing
can be lost and everything is gained.

I used to tell stories. Things swelled,
and crested. In a word, they ended.
But when the spiders rolled out after you,
they took the endings away.
No sunsets and no after. Only holes
strung together, a succession of lacks
between the Zenith and the willow-ware,
their blue patterns stretching off
into nights that open over me like an orange,
its sections more spacious than any story,
too expansive for an ending to take.

What if I could cure and keep
our one sad slice of time? When noon's
harsh flash throws the river into duotone,
we'll finally be fixed in place, shining
as the instant stretches out. In the next slide,
mustachioed men crow over bumper crops
of oranges, captions scrawled across their torsos.
Then the biggest fish, the departing ship,
our house decaying hourly into landscape—
each picture a proof of the island's treasured curse:
the things that fail are the only things that stay.

ACKNOWLEDGMENTS

Thank you to the friends who read and commented on this book as it took shape: Shanna Compton, Anne Gorrick, Kate Greenstreet, Shafer Hall, Kaplan Harris, Barbara Heritage, erica kaufman, Jennifer L. Knox, Jessica Smith, and Logan Ryan Smith. Your help was invaluable.

Thank you to the journals that have published portions of this manuscript, sometimes in different forms: *Barrelhouse*, *Coconut*, *A Handsome Journal*, *The Hat*, *Hot Whiskey*, *Hotel Amerika*, *LIT*, *LOCUSPOINT*, *Listenlight*, *Poor Claudia*, *So-and-So*, and *String of Small Machines*. Thanks especially to Sandra Beasley, Dan Brady, Jordan Davis, Reb Livingston, and Ada Limón, in their capacities editorial and otherwise, for supporting my work.

Thanks also to the members of the DC poetry community for their friendship and encouragement, particularly Buck Downs, Cathy Eisenhower, Mel Nichols, Rod Smith, and Ryan Walker.

Many thanks to Matvei Yankelevich, Anna Moschovakis, David Jou, and everyone at Ugly Duckling Presse for all their hard work and for their belief in this project.

Thanks again and always to Jeffrey Eaton, for giving more than I dared to ask.

ABOUT THE AUTHOR

Maureen Thorson is a poet, publisher, and book designer living in Washington, DC. She is the author of the chapbooks *Twenty Questions for the Drunken Sailor*, *Mayport*, and *Novelty Act*, among others. She is the publisher and editor of Big Game Books, a small press dedicated to emerging poets. Maureen is the co-curator of the In Your Ear reading series at the D.C. Arts Center and the founder of NaPoWriMo, an annual project in which poets attempt to write a poem a day for the month of April. *Applies to Oranges* is her first full-length book.

COLOPHON

Applies to Oranges
by Maureen Thorson
First Edition, First Printing 2011
1,100 copies

This book designed by *wysiwyg*
with text set in Bembo.

Books printed on partially-recycled
FSC-certified paper by McNaughton & Gunn.

Covers letterpress-printed on Oxford paper
at the Ugly Duckling Presse studio with
seventy-five copies signed and numbered
as part of a limited collector's edition
with a letterpress broadside.

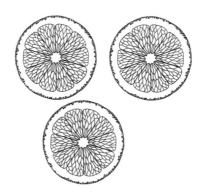